A Thousand Silent Thoughts

Kerri Elliot

BookLeaf
Publishing

India | USA | UK

Presentation by *BookLeaf Publishing*

Web: www.bookleafpub.com

E-mail: info@bookleafpub.com

ISBN: 9789357446839

First edition 2022

DEDICATION

For Samantha, whose knowledge of beauty and the world knew no bounds, I live my life in part for you.

For Danny, whose inspiration taught me it could be done.

For Sarah, you show me what I could possibly achieve.

For James, who showed enough belief and wonder to make me carry on.

ACKNOWLEDGEMENT

I could spend my life thanking people to be honest, I am surrounded my so much love and support from family and friends that its a wonder I don't reach out every night and touch the stars.

Thank you to my Husband who supports me in my craziest dreams but grounds me in reality so I don't float away.

Thank you to my Dad who has spent his life helping me to never lose my faith in magic.

And especially

Thank you to my mum, you fought these battles with me, every single one. Without you I don't know how I'd have survived.

I love you all.

PREFACE

My dream for many years has been to write a book, its strange how long it took me to make the leap from reading to writing but once I got there I didn't know how to stop. Poetry is particularly close to my heart because its never been something that I have sat down and set out to do. It was something that one day started pouring out of me and never really stopped. I have never written my poetry with any sort of form in mind and I never edit it. It's raw nature is a big part of what makes it special for me. To some it may seem disjointed and uncoordinated (a bit like I am) but really it is raw and pure and I believe that the people who can see that are the people who will understand it.

You

You are not a delicate little flower;
You are every flower in the forest blooming at
once.
You are overwhelming.
You are not a snowflake, though as unique,
You are an entire avalanche.
You are not a single raindrop, falling down my
cheek;
You are an entire thunderstorm.
You are a cataclysm.
The earth does not spin beneath your feet,
turning as it will
You move the earth,
the whole world turns on your axis.
The moon does not control the tides,
they ebb and flow to your will.
My world no longer revolves around the sun,
It now orbits you.

Hiding

Did you know that there's a monster hiding
underneath my bed
He comes out in the night time and whispers
stories in my head

Did you know that there's a dragon hiding deep
within my heart
He comes out when I am afraid breathing fire in
the dark

Did you know there is a poet hiding well inside
my soul
Singing sweet soft words to me to keep my spirit
whole

Did you know there is a demon hiding deep
inside my brain
Sometimes he sits there quietly and others
inflicts pain

Did you know there is a mermaid hiding
underneath my feet
She's always there to ground me when my
thoughts get way too deep

Did you know there is me that's hiding right in front of you
I'm not surprised you didn't, only I can see her too.

The Girl

Once upon a time
A girl turned 10
Not knowing she was heading
To a lion's den

Constant battles
Uphill all the way
What was next
No one could say

The girl kept fighting
Year after year
The hardness increasing
Always in fear

But still she fought
Kept going on
Still not knowing
What was to come

Once upon a time
A girl fell in love
An angel was sent
To her from above

He joined in her battles
Fought the good fight
Then watched over her sleeping
All through the night

She still had her wars
A difficult life
Her sanity balanced
On edge of a knife

But her love he kept her
Safe sane and sound
Kept right by her side
Kept her feet on the ground

Her love he did save her
Though the battles don't stop
His loves the only
Good thing that she's got

Darkness

I'm trying to tell a story
I don't know where to start
But soon it all comes flooding out
The words ripped from my heart

This story is a sad one
As all great stories are
As long as you're not living it
Just reading from afar

But trapped inside this story
My world is a mess
I'm constantly surround
By sorrow and by stress

I feel in time just maybe
It all will take a break
As soon as I can touch it
A chance I'll have to take

There's got to be some out there
Some happiness for me
I can't just be a construct
I'll never get to see

So I will keep on hoping
And reaching out for it
One day I'll find the happy
And keep a little bit
I watch the darkness coming
Closing in above my head
It blankets out the sunshine
While I lie here in my bed

My memories forgotten
My mind is now asleep
I drift off very peacefully
My thoughts no longer deep

But there are little lights there
Shining brightly from the sky
Glowing very softly
While here I simply lie

Are they dreams or are they stars
Shining up there in the night
Slipping in and out of focus
In the darkness glowing white

I do not fear the darkness
There is light just shining through
Always watching over me
And watching over you

Happiness

I'm trying to tell a story
I don't know where to start
But soon it all comes flooding out
The words ripped from my heart

This story is a sad one
As all great stories are
As long as you're not living it
Just reading from afar

But trapped inside this story
My world is a mess
I'm constantly surround
By sorrow and by stress

I feel in time just maybe
It all will take a break
As soon as I can touch it
A chance I'll have to take

There's got to be some out there
Some happiness for me
I can't just be a construct
I'll never get to see

So I will keep on hoping
And reaching out for it
One day I'll find the happy
And keep a little bit

Happy

I thought that once I knew
What my life was going to be
It seemed a simple thing
I just want to be happy

Sometimes I am
And sometimes not
It tends not to be easy
To live the life you want to live
I just want to be happy

I reach and grasp and try to hold
Onto the good around me
But sometimes it just slips out of reach
Into the world surrounding
But try I must, what else to do
I just want to be happy

There's good things there
And bad things here
It was never to be easy
Try and try and try again
I just want to be happy

I think one day I'll catch it though

And hold on oh so tightly
I'll have it then and not let go
I'll finally be happy

My Stars

My head is split wide open
and out spill all the stars
Collect them all up one by one
 and trap them all in jars
But hopes are ever changing
They cannot be contained
My wishes overflow the lip
Where you think you have them chained
You cannot keep my dreams
Though tightly as you hold
They'll flow and travel back to me
No matter what I'm told
My dreams will live forever
My hopes and wishes too
Stop trying to claim mine now
Your dreams belong to you.

Emotions

I cannot find the words
I don't know where to start
How do I find a way to calm
My restless beating heart
My minds a whirlwind of thoughts
I don't know where to begin
To sort out my emotions
That are tumultuous within
My heart is beating faster
Every second that does pass
It's going to beat right out my chest
if I do not calm it fast
Are my emotions in my head
or are they beating with my heart
I'm trying to control them
but I'm just falling apart

Existing

If I sit here in the silence
Am I making any sound

Is my heart still in there beating
Is there life still all around

If I sit here never moving
Do I still take in a breath

Is it moving in my lungs
Pushing in and out my chest

If I sit here never thinking
Are my thoughts still even there

If I simply stopped existing
Would the world even care

The Star

A star up sparkling in the sky
Lights up the night til it shall die
When the darkness does descend
You beg the star to be your friend
Let its light drive away your fears
Dries up all those wrung out tears
But once the sun comes out in day
You tell the star to go away
The sun lights up your precious world
Your bright white life now sees no trouble
No longer needs the stars clear light
To help you make it through the night
The star sails back to sky above
Flapping like a bright white dove
Tears the star itself now sheds
While you sleep sound in your beds
The star it weeps without your need
No one's happiness to feed
Its job is done and no one cares
In the darkness it was there.

5 Steps

She stood up.
Stood up and took one wobbling, shaking step
forward.
Her face twisted in pain and tears streamed
down her face but she walked, slowly and
carefully and painfully towards me.
I watched her twisted mangled feet as they
struggled to hold her up.
She had no semblance of balance and there was
fire in her eyes shining out at me.
I could see the fire in her eyes as it mimicked the
pain that I knew danced up and down her legs,
but she kept walking, getting closer and closer to
me as I froze in awe of her.
We had switched places.
Here I was frozen still unable to move my feet,
unable to comprehend what I was seeing as she
moved,
as she stood,
as she placed one foot in front of the other
and walked 5 steps.

RSD

Sparks fly up and down her limbs
Searing pure white flesh
But because you cannot see it
You assume it's in her head
The fire dances in her eyes
The only glimpse you'll find
Of the pain she always feels inside
That she tries so hard to hide
Little tears fall from her eyes
But nothing can they do
To put out the hot white fire
That's burning straight on through
Her eyes hold pain you can't describe
Her whole world is on fire
What if just one day those flames
 Become a funeral pyre
A heat so hot that can't be stopped
It's going to burn her out
Her strength for this is failing
Her time is running out.

I wait

I wait
I sit in the dark and wait

I wonder what is coming

Though I do not know what it is
I wait for it

I wait
Believing that it is coming

I wait

The Monster

Have a told you there's a monster hiding
underneath my bed,
he whispers in the night to me all the dark
thoughts in my head.
He sets my mind on fire and burns my walls
down to the ground,
his words they slowly strangle me when I should
be sleeping sound.
The monster lives so deeply in the corners of my
brain,
picking memories and thoughts apart and using
them for pain.
He knows my every secret, every thought and
every word,
my mind is his destruction zone where I am
trapped like a caged bird.
Listening all the night long as he softly sings to
me,
of pain and fear and awful things,
A haunting melody.
Until the dawn is breaking he just rattles all
around,
causing devastation where he then cannot be
found.

Have I told you there's a monster hiding in my
mind,
that if I look into a mirror, in my eyes he I shall
find.

Hole

There's a hole here in my body where I know
that you should be
But missing from my arms now is a face I'll
never see
I'll never get to see you smile
Or just look up at me
You were taken from me quickly
Told it wasn't meant to be
But the hole you left it lingers
In my chest and in my heart
It won't fill up with memories
We didn't get to start

But in my heads a knowledge
I know that you were there
No one can take that from me
They wouldn't even dare

I'll hold on to you tightly
Keep you close and keep you near
Until one day my angel
Your sweet voice I know I'll hear

So live the life you have now
Play among the stars

A know my little angel
I am watching from afar

One day

I dreamed to hold you closely
Learn a face I never knew
I loved you oh so dearly
Felt my life was starting new
But dreams can't last forever
Every one they have to end
So my life with you faded away
A wound that will not mend
One day I will be with you
A new start I hope we get
The pain of loving someone
You never even met

Loss

I watched as you faded away
Across an open field
My heart was slowly breaking
While your soul had finally healed
Your footprints turned to dust
Getting lost among the stars
Your loss it left a mark on me
A heart now full of scars
But your image never faded from my heart or
from my mind
I see you each and everyday walking by my side
I feel your warm bright presence
Linger by when I am down
It brings me so much comfort though you do not
make a sound

Blood

I clean the blood off of the walls and the blood
off of the floors.
I scrub and scrub the blood away from inside of
our own doors.
We tell ourselves you didn't mean it, that you
were sad afraid or scared.
We tell ourselves it all again in case one day we
aren't there.
What if we went out one day instead of watching
you?
What if when we then came back and there was
nothing we could do.
Clean it all, remove the blood is if it didn't
happen.
Do it all again next time and try to keep you
happy.

While my sister sleeps

I really have to tell you now you're making me quite scared.
I don't know what to do now I'm crying on the stairs.

I'm scared you're going to leave me and I can't do a thing.
Cause hell is here on earth for you and you wish to have wings.

If I could make it go away I'd have done it long before.
I'd have made it go away when you first hit the floor.

I'm really scared I don't know how to make this go away.
I can't imagine how you feel every single day.

You say you want to leave the world but I wish that you could see.

If you're going to leave the world then you're
also leaving me.

I don't want to be without you your part of my
very soul.
But I can't make it better when you're feeling so
so low.

I try to wipe the blood away and pretend it
wasn't there.
But I wake up every morning terrified and
scared.

I'm really scared to check now I'm really scared
to see.
Have you now done something else that's going
to make you bleed.

I'm sitting by your door now I'm sitting in the
dark.
I'm hoping that you're sleeping and not falling
apart.

I'm trying hard to tell you now I'm trying to
make you see.
That if you kill yourself. Your killing part of me.

www.ingramcontent.com/pod-product-compliance
Lightning Source LLC
LaVergne TN
LVHW021329200726
843509LV00014B/2448